AN IRISH HEART

Poetic Memoirs of a Belfast Child

Greg McVicker, BSW.

Copyright © 2017 by Greg McVicker
Second Published Edition - April 2019.
Cover Photo by Ballygally View Images.
Cover and Layout by Trevor Harper & Greg McVicker.

All rights reserved.

No part of this publication may be reproduced in any form, or by any means, electronic or mechanical, including photocopying, recording, or any information browsing, storing, or retrieval system, without permission in writing from the publisher.

ISBN
978-1-989053-17-1 (Softcover)
978-1-7751622-1-6 (eBook)

Produced by:
Belfast Child Publishing

Table of Contents

Introduction	4
Stranger to my Land	6
Knockagh Monument	10
Scattered Youth	16
Hallows' Eve	20
An Ode to my Aunt Sadie	24
Belfast Craic	28
Whispers in the Breeze	32
Cry of the Wild	36
The Enchantment of Achill	40
Alcohol Saviour	46
C'est La Vie	50
Little Angel	54
Hearts Entwined	62
Imagine That…	66
Empty Promises	70
Going Forward in Reverse	74
A New Beginning	78
The Pulse of Derrylin	84
Mum's Lament	90
Lament for a Child	96
Surreal, Nine One One	100
Bruised and Battered	104
Disposable Human	110
The Confessional	114
Acknowledgements	118
Other Titles from Greg McVicker	121
Connect with the Author	127

Introduction

In the 1980's, a trio of brothers from the small farming community of Derrylin, County Fermanagh, traded in their traditional Irish instruments and would go on to form one of Northern Ireland's most powerful and successful rock bands: **Mama's Boys**. The music as created by **Pat, John, and Tommy McManus** instills as much inspiration today as the day it was first unleashed to their faithful global following, including me.

As a result, and for years, I tried writing songs inspired by these musical geniuses, since they had left the deepest, and most profound of impacts, upon my eager mind. No matter how hard I tried, however, my compositions would end up in poetic format.

As my hand at songwriting failed, some of the poems were created with guidance from my beloved mum, **Catherine McVicker**, who departed from this world on May 11, 2005. Her memoir can be seen within '**Mum's Lament**'; her full story is captured through a personal reflection of the same name and appears within my first published book: '**Through the Eyes of a Belfast Child: Life. Personal Reflections. Poems.**' It speaks to my mum's undying love, dedication, and concerted efforts to protect her four asthmatic children throughout one of the most, darkest periods, during Ireland's brutal history, often referred to as *'The Troubles.'* Her story tells that a mother's love knows no boundaries, even during her own time under a veil of death's calling.

Since publishing Belfast Child, a wonderful colleague of mine, **Henrietta Pratt**, suggested that I put all of my poems forth into their own book. Each poem is penned using a storytelling format, speaking to life-changing events that everyone can relate to and reflect upon.

As I often say, "In life, we all have a cross to bear and a very unique story to tell; we just hope that someone will take the time to listen."

So here we are… thank you for taking that time.

Stranger to my Land

Photo by: Ciarán McVicker

"We were on the upper level balcony, and as the building shook from the shockwave created by the bombing, we screamed. In our state of panic, we tried to get up and run, along with every other patron caught in this explosion. My dad threw his body over the four of us with his arms and legs fully outstretched, pinning us to the seats while saying, "Stay down and don't move. You don't go outside, as there might be a second one waiting for you." What he was referencing is that once the first explosion had gone off and had created its intended shock, panic, and chaos, a second device was usually planted and packed with glass, barbed wire, nails, and shrapnel, to cause as much human devastation as possible."

Through the Eyes of a Belfast Child, page 43.

Stranger to my Land

In my beloved town of Belfast,
Off goes yet another devastating bomb blast.
In the streets the people lie dying,
Over their bodies, their families start crying.

In a land that is run by hatred and rule,
Fragile people are made to feel like a fool.
Where the citizen's would like to have the choice,
Freedom of speech, the language in their voice.

Both sides, for their marches and silly parades,
Look like nothing more than a game of charades.
While they walk so defiant, they chant and they shout,
"Soon we will get all of those other bastards out."

While we know the place is well overrun,
By ignorance, who shall hide behind a gun.
They target all innocence that lock into sight,
They continue their torture by day and by night.

When people do apply for a job,
Noses are turned up just like a snob.
"We will only hire from our own kind,
You're fully qualified, but not what we had in mind."

There are many armies that walk the street,
They point their guns at certain people they meet.
They know whose side that they will take,
Their sincerity can be determined as nothing but fake.

To the people that live on the non-sectarian road,
When they ask for assistance, they are left in the cold.
The safeguards that were put into place,
Will shower them with bullets and spit in their face.

I wonder if my country will try and make peace,
Will the guns stay silent? Will the violence cease?
Will people no longer hide behind a frown?
Will they finally have freedom from the bitterness they drown?

My closing word to the nations of the Emerald Isle:
Hold your heads high, and be proud when you smile.
Now is the time for the healing seeds to grow,
Give a chance to be united, and not for what you know.

"It seemed that Knockagh stood guard over our neighbourhood in Knockview. As far back as I can remember, while playing out in the garden with Karen, Joe, and Angela, we could simply look over and see this magnificent structure behind us while pondering what dark and haunting secrets it held. We would get a hold of our dad's binoculars and peer at this memorial with curiosity and awe, although I never truly knew why it was there or what it meant. This was a symbol up on the mountain that looked out below to the permanently spoiled lands of "The Troubles" and the wars that raged for so long across Northern Ireland."

Through the Eyes of a Belfast Child, page 35.

Knockagh Monument

For many a day,
And plenty of years.
You watched over my house,
Your shadow showed no fears.

Across the valley,
And up on the hill.
You stood there, so peaceful,
Incredibly still.

I would look out the window,
My eyes ablaze.
My focus entranced,
Feeling like I was dazed.

Like a soldier to attention,
You stood on your guard.
Looking out over Newtownabbey,
Surrounding fields so scarred.

Then the time, it did come,
One warm and sunny day.
My brother took my hand,
And he showed me the way.

So with this spellbound visit,
To the place we watched from afar.
My brother and I would venture,
Without the use of a car.

On our matching Choppers,
Our legs pedaled a pace.
We found the journey to be difficult,
With the wind caught in our face.

With our little hearts so eager,
Yet our wills determined, so strong.
We would come to face you,
Although the journey was quite long.

The narrow roads we followed,
Would take a twist or turn.
Because we cycled so hard,
Our muscles started to burn.

We would not stop very often,
Even to catch a breath.
Our curiosity kept us wanting,
To view the Memorial of Death.

When we reached the top of the hill,
Our journey almost complete,
We tasted the victory of a champion,
We would not smell defeat.

We embarked upon that final leg,
The road that tried to beat thee.
Now we would cheer in glorious shouts,
As we took ourselves to one knee.

With fire in our eyes,
Yet a passionate stare.
We focused on your might,
As bold as we did dare.

We read the names of,
The people who were so brave.
They put down their lives in world wars,
Sending their courage to an early grave.

Now in your shadow we stand tall,
And still we show no fear.
For now we know the purpose,
Of why you have been placed here.

We looked out across the valley,
To the house where we play ball.
It's funny now seeing you incredibly huge,
And our grand home so small.

For when we look at you each day,
You look not so big in might,
We can close you between our fingers,
And knock view out of sight.

Now that we have had the chance,
Standing upon your sacred ground.
We know that we can be rest assured,
You'll gaze at us year round.

Photo by: Caitlin McVicker

Scattered Youth

Photo by: Florian Pircher

"Suddenly I found myself surrounded by girls who wanted to hear me speak to them. Although I'd ask them to engage me in a conversation for sake of interaction, they would simply reply, "Just talk" from which I would lose interest. I'd point out they themselves had strong accents but they disagreed with my statement. On the other hand, guys would try to impersonate me but sounded ridiculous. In their own minds, while trying to be funny they thought they were the next best thing to sliced bread. In their ignorance, they'd tell me to speak English, learn how to talk properly or to get back on the boat I came from and go back to my own country in the mockery of my voice."

        Through the Eyes of a Belfast Child, page 19.

Scattered Youth

Recollecting my thoughts,
Of the years gone by.
Looking back to my childhood,
Heavy-breathed, I sigh.

I think of my friends,
And the places we played.
The secrets we kept,
The promises we made.

I reflect on the words,
To each other we'd say.
Tomorrow is our future,
Which now was yesterday.

With each morning that shone,
With every passing star.
Always there for one another,
We would never stray far.

Passing by along the street,
In our land of the Emerald Isle.
No matter our inner mood,
We managed to crack a smile.

Friendships were more than special,
We knew more than just a name.
Together we fought hard as one,
Never experiencing guilt or shame.

I thought our happiness would never end,
Through the days and years we'd seen.
Now fifteen years on down the line,
In a different country I've been.

Letters and calls once abundant,
Have all but come to a halt.
Should we say that being divided,
Is where we could lay fault?

We all have gone our separate ways,
New lives they have begun.
Anticipating one day we all reunite,
Before our final song is sung.

"We hoped that when the homeowner answered he or she would see a headless horseman, although we did not have a horse to accompany us. We thought our gimmick was brilliant and deserved a gold medal. Others, however, and specifically the homeowner (whose time we were obviously wasting) told us we were too cheap to buy a plastic Halloween mask at the Woodford shops for 10p. Their assumptions were very much correct, as we were often met with, "Ack, wee lads, will ye take yerselves off by the hawn and quit wastin' my time for flips sake.""

>Through the Eyes of a Belfast Child, page 50.

Hallows' Eve

The leaves, they all have fallen,
Final destination is the ground.
As the wind breezes through so gently,
The decay jumps to life with sound.

Darkness has cloaked the earth,
Yet no child will show a frown.
For this moment, it's not time for bed,
Instead they'll awaken the town.

The pumpkins are all carved,
Eagerly waiting to be lit.
Boldly taking their lifeless places,
On the porchways where they sit.

Witches pass by shrieking,
Ghosts, they whisper boo.
Doing the very best they can,
To frighten the life right out of you.

The children are all in costume,
Their hands wishing for a treat.
Along the path to every house,
They shuffle their anxious feet.

When they reach the doorway,
The moon is shining through.
Make sure that you fill every bag,
Or they might play a trick on you.

Listen to the neighbourhood,
And the laughter that fills the air.
"Trick or treat" surprises you quick,
It's a two-foot grizzly bear.

Celebrating the ritual of Hallows' Eve,
Illuminated by moonlight.
Children of all shapes and sizes,
Will appear at your door tonight.

As this evening draws to a close,
The zombies have gone back to their tomb.
Take a glance towards the night sky,
And capture a witch flying out on her broom.

"In following the tradition of many an Irish family, my cousins planned a get-together after the funeral and had a celebration for my aunt's life. Prior to going I had decided to try my hand at eulogizing her. I listened as my mum told me about how my aunt and uncle got together and what they did to ensure their happiness against the wishes of many. I captured those words and shared them with my cousins who were present."

Through the Eyes of a Belfast Child, page 65.

An Ode to my Aunt Sadie

Sarah Anne Corbett was once a wee woman,
Who came from the land of the green.
Along came my Uncle John,
And she became his beauty queen.

Off to England, they did run,
And husband & wife they became.
Although some gave not their blessing,
They married all the same.

That magical day they did elope,
Must have been a match made in heaven.
For only a handful of people knew,
That she was now called Sadie Devlin.

Their love for each other grew stronger each day,
And five young children would appear.
John, Sarah, Maria, Jim, and the saintly one, Patrick,
Their ages each separated by a year.

From Belfast to Canada, the family did come,
And a new life it would start.
My wee Auntie Sadie,
Loved Uncle John with all her heart.

My wee auntie Sadie had quite the Irish brogue,
And another thing I'll tell ya, her heart was made of gold.
Her kindness, compassion, her love and forgiveness,
Would never ever turn cold.

The warmth in her smile, the gleam in her eyes,
The way she said, "Oh Frig."
My wee auntie Sadie always did prefer a headbang,
Over a good wee Irish jig.

Aunt Sadie's favourite song,
Was "Spirit In The Sky."
And with that spirit she now is with,
That no one can deny.

So to my wee aunt Sadie,
Here's to us and "frig" the rest.
It definitely is a blessing to know,
You are one of the very best!

There's No Such Word As Can't. Craic and Banter.
Face Like A Lurgan Spade.
Good Auld Spud. Ack, Yer Ballicks!
How's Yer Arse For Love Bites? The Money Man's Dead.
Dirty Hallion! Wind Yer Neck In!
Hit A Redner. So I Am.
Friggin' Steamin'.
So It Is. Sure Nah.
Quit Pickin' Yer Willick. Up Joe's Hole In America.
Yer Head's Cut.
Take A Wisner.
Frig Away Off. 'Mere I Tell You Sumthin'.
Wee Millie. Bake Like A Busted Sausage.
Buck Eejit.
Away And Kiss One Of Me Arses!
Spit The Dummy Out!
Sound As A Pound.
Ack, Me Arse!
Ack, Yer Ma! Wise The Bap.
Yer Full Of Shite.
That's Boggin'. The Snatter's Are Trippin' Ye! What's The Craic?
Yer Ma's Yer Da!
If You Don't Like It, Lump It!
Ack, Aye. Wee Lad. Happy Days.
Catch Yerself On! So You Are.
Steal My Grave As Quick?
I'll Put My Toe Up Yer Hole!
Bloody Blootered.
Dead On. Pollaxed. Bog Roll.
Give My Head Peace! Dig In The Gub?
Bout Ye, Mucker? Auld Doll.
Friggin' Wee Shite! Dirty Baste.

Greg McVicker

"After making their way around to where the wake is being held, they ask, "Is this where the dead man lives?" Once confirmed, they offer sincerest condolences, and give a few words of how the deceased would be sorely missed, while making up a load of complete and utter shite as to how they knew that person. They would then proceed with their original intent to have a few pints, a couple of sandwiches, and a jaffa cake or two at the expense of the grieving relatives."

Through the Eyes of a Belfast Child, page 100.

Belfast Craic

A toast with a pint of Guinness,
Is how we raise a jar.
And if we talk about the boot,
We mean the trunk of a car.

If we say he's blootered,
What we're saying is he's drunk.
To say that something's boggin',
We're saying that it stunk.

If you're told to shut yer gub,
It's better not to talk.
And if we tell you to take a hike,
It's not a mountain walk.

If you're told to go and shite,
That does not mean the bathroom calls.
But if we ask where to find a bog,
We need the toilet stalls.

If you're asked "What's the craic?"
Have you any news to tell?
If you've a face like a busted sausage,
It means you're as ugly as hell.

If told you're a buck eejit,
We mean you're a nutcase.
If your bake looks like a Lurgan spade,
You're looking really long in the face.

When told something's dead on,
It must be really good.
When told to take yourself off by the hand,
You've put me in a bad mood.

When told to put the fire on,
It means a shovel of coal.
If you don't do what you're told,
You'll get my toe up your hole.

Whispers in the Breeze

Photo by: Enrique Meseguer

"Lost in a trance that day as I gazed at their headstone, it suddenly dawned on me I was following a process that many others do. People from all around this world, regardless of age, race, culture, or religious background, enter into the same processes and reflect upon the lives of their beloved family members. There I stood in a lonely graveyard, reminiscing on the lives once shared before their untimely passing."

Through the Eyes of a Belfast Child, page 71.

Whispers in the Breeze

Realizing my innermost fears,
Choking back the steady stream of tears.
Not knowing your time had come,
Without you I feel so numb.

Just a whisper in the breeze,
Brought my world down to its knees.
The day that you were called away,
Paradise is where you now stay.

When the days do come to pass,
I call upon your bed of grass.
Comfort inside knowing you're there,
Looking up at my vacant stare.

The silence I exchange with thee,
Speaks volumes, I'm sure this you'll see.
My shadow casts across your grave,
While I stand so lonely, I stand so brave.

Now the days they seem so long,
In your arms is where I belong.
I close my eyes and hear you speak,
You call my name; my legs feel weak.

Together we promised that we would grow old,
We thought our happiness would never unfold.
I kneel at your feet with my head hung low,
Thoughts in my mind you already know.

This quality time with you I spend,
Will hopefully help my broken heart mend.
Feeling guilty when I turn to leave,
Returning home I continue to grieve.

When my term approaches death,
Time to exhale one final breath.
I wonder if others will fall to their knees,
When my name whispers in the breeze.

Cry of the Wild

Photo by: Patrice Audet

"The difference between our cultures and the destruction of our language is that I never received mine until age twelve, while Indigenous people had theirs removed from them at an even earlier age. My language was beaten into me and molested into other students, while it was also sexually violated and beaten out of the Indigenous people through horrific and inhumane actions and deeds after being forcefully sent to attend the Indian Residential School system."

Through the Eyes of a Belfast Child, page 172.

Cry of the Wild

I am of one spirit, placed upon this earth,
My parents were chosen long before my birth.
For now while I grow, I have begun to see,
The animal instinct that lies so deep within me.

The wolf is a creature that is misunderstood,
They say it just hunts for shelter and food.
My own wolf within is my guiding light,
Who protects me from darkness, predators, and fright.

The wolf within teaches me how to survive,
The wolf within uses all senses, there's five.
Touch, taste, smell, hearing, and sight,
The wolf within helps me to fight.

In a world where mankind will steal from his kin,
After the Creator lay down to forgive us from sin.
My wolf from my soul will know not to stray,
My wolf keeps me protected with each brand new day.

You stay by my side with each step that I take,
You protect me forever; your pride you don't fake.
I will listen so intently and hear when you cry,
You'll never abandon me when my time comes to die.

When my sanity is low and I have lost track,
I will call to my wolf, who runs with his pack.
The animal inside me will rear up his head,
Warning those who will harm me, they'd be better off dead.

When I close my eyes and lay me down to sleep,
I have prayed to the Creator for my soul to keep.
Deep inside my flame burns, my wolf he keeps care,
For my spirit, so strong, he keeps from despair.

If you take a good look at yourself inside,
You too shall find an animal with pride.
It might be an eagle, a wolf, a bear, or a deer,
Who will keep you from danger, protect you from fear.

So tomorrow, look around you, and you shall soon find,
There has been an animal given to each of mankind.
This animal will guide you to the white pearly gate,
Teach you how to forgive, and lead you from hate.

Photo by: Anthony

"To my understanding, this is where one of the darkest parts of Irish history is hidden. It is often referred to as "The Great Famine." I understand this was actually a starvation of the Irish by absentee British land agents who charged outrageous amounts of money for land but also took food raised by locals and gave it to their lords for their own survival. Regardless of the potato blight that occurred, other crops were available that the Irish could use, including food from livestock such as goats milk."

Through the Eyes of a Belfast Child, page 76.

The Enchantment of Achill

The journey began on a long winding road,
This day of adventure was about to unfold.
The car, it did stop at the foot of the hill,
My heart, it beat fast; I could hardly sit still.

I stood in amazement at the Celtic gravesite,
Which watched over our ancestors by day and by night.
And now their village I would carefully explore,
But how was I to know I would discover so much more?

I ascended the slope, my eyes they sat wide,
With the beauty around me I was filled with such pride.
But all of a sudden things they would change,
Was I going mad, or could I be strange?

My ears, they perked up at the wonderful sound,
Of Irish war pipes, but they were nowhere to be found.
I scanned the horizon; I looked left and right,
I looked all around, but still no one was in sight.

I turned to my aunt and asked her the same,
"Can you hear the war pipes that now roam in my brain?"
"I hear them indeed," was her reply to me,
"Do not be afraid; let your spirit roam free."

I let myself relax and began to feel at peace,
The pipes of great sadness then seemed to cease.
I cleared up my mind and focused my gaze,
The sheep were not bothered; they continued to graze.

I stood at the village, which was once full of life,
Until Captain Boycott came, so bitter with strife.
He worked those poor people and left them in vain,
"You'll work in the sunlight; you'll work in the rain."

My legs walked easily into each of the homes,
My hands traced freely, touching each of the stones.
I stood in these ruins with such delicate care,
My ancestors of the past watched over my stare.

The others, they left and descended the hill,
My spirit was strong, and so was my will.
I put down my camera and closed my eyes,
And boy was I in for a major surprise.

I brought up my left hand to cover my face,
And felt those good souls lift me to their place.
Cast back to their day when their lives were so free,
They were such a proud people; this was easy to see.

*I heard words of excitement escape from my throat,
I watched in awe, and this I do quote.
"Making food, harvesting land, with not one penny to pay,
Tending to sheep, milking goats, we will survive another day."*

*I felt a great rush sweep right though my soul,
My spirit quickly ignited, I totally felt whole.
By these ancestors of ours who worked hard on the land,
Brought me to their era, and amongst them I did stand.*

*When the time, it did come, for me to move down,
Back to the Celtic gravesites, I thought I might frown.
But when I reflected on my experience back a short mile,
I thanked my ancestors for making me smile.*

*They opened my soul and my spirit so deep,
They strengthened my flame, which was so weak.
They brought me back without any wrath,
So that I might complete my journey and my path.*

*In this life in which I have been placed,
I carry the torch, I carry the faith.
For those who are down and feel right out,
I share all my energies to remove all their doubt.*

So if with this poem you may chance to read,
Plant the next positive energy of life-giving seed.
Before you give up and close the door,
Think of my ancestors and the cross that they bore.

Photo by: Greg McVicker

Alcohol Saviour

Photo by: Khusen Rustamov

"She explained that there was usually more than one involved in the savage events that occurred each time. She went on to say that some believed her addiction to alcohol and outward displays while under the influence led them to believe she offered herself as a reward for them feeding her desire for more booze. I never asked, but wondered if anyone had stopped to ask why they felt they had a rite of passage to her body. Whatever the case may be, she found a way to survive, as do many others who walk in her shoes. She was not and is not alone in her journey."

Through the Eyes of a Belfast Child, page 160.

Alcohol Saviour

Won't you take a look at me?
Enjoy my perfect outer shell.
Before you discover what's inside,
You'd be better to run like hell.

You enter my life so undoubting,
As I display my pretty face.
Satisfy me with sambuca and beer,
Then conquer my body space.

The mask you find upon my eyes,
Does not cover all of my scars.
For every day that I leave work,
My conscience is attracted to bars.

This poison that I take within,
Is what keeps my inferno alive.
Without my bottle of liquid fuel,
How else would I survive?

To myself this awful addiction,
Will see me through the day.
All I need is one more drink,
Yet I have no credit to pay.

Friends feed my desire for more substances,
Placing myself into an unconscious state.
They take me upstairs to my safe haven,
Without remorse, they begin to violate.

Turning once again to the chalice,
Realizing it's my only true friend.
Now I slip into a downward spiral,
My numb body does descend.

My children, they sleep so peacefully,
For they are unaware of what I do.
Contemplating suicide in drunken stupor,
Three times, I have not followed through.

Although I have told you my secret,
I have considered you my soul mate.
Please move on without me,
Before you find it's too late.

Photo by: Stefan Keller

"We create differing levels of society and try to impose our belief systems onto other cultures by telling them that in order to be human, they have to be more like us. Who are we to dictate the creation of life when we ourselves are not perfect? It's easy to say treat all humans equally and be kind to one another, but that has never been the case."

    Through the Eyes of a Belfast Child, page 152.

C'est La Vie

Have you ever tried to shout out loud,
But you have forgotten how to scream.
Have you ever tried to fall asleep,
When you are already in a dream.

Have you ever tried to run away,
But you have no idea how to walk.
Have you ever tried to have a conversation,
When you know not how to talk.

Have you ever tried to read a book,
But you have lost your sense of sight.
Have you ever tried to climb a mountain,
When you know your fear of height.

Have you ever wanted to visit your past,
But you have no clue where you've been.
Have you ever tried to hide your face,
When you're crowned a beauty queen.

Have you ever tried to stop the bleeding,
But you never received a cut.
Have you ever wanted to lie down and die,
When your coffin has already been shut.

Have you ever tried to place a wager,
But you haven't a penny to bet.
Have you ever tried to love someone,
When you've never even met.

Have you ever looked at yourself in a mirror,
But don't recognize what you see.
Have you ever tried to say you're fine,
When your body is in agony.

Have you ever tried to have a laugh,
But all you ever do is cry.
Have you ever tried to kiss the moon,
When you have no wings to fly.

Have you ever wanted to change the world,
But you don't know what it should be.
Have you never realized these things happen for a reason,
When the truth is C'est La Vie.

Little Angel

Photo by: Sally Wynn

"Being a dad is no easy feat. It takes a great amount of dedication and responsibility to step up to the plate when bringing a child into the world. It takes someone with determination to face the unknown. In being a first-time father, having never held a baby in their arms before and with no instruction manual to guide one through the multitude of steps that it takes to raise a child, one has to learn what they were taught from their parents."

Through the Eyes of a Belfast Child, page 185.

Little Angel

I know a young lad from a local town,
In these last few years, he has done nothing but frown.
His life, it has changed from bad to worse,
It seems unto him there has been placed a curse.

He married a girl, he was happy and all,
In the first few years they had such a ball.
Now as he reflects on the years gone by,
There is only one person for whom he would die.

Her name is important; his daughter is she,
She filled up his life with musical harmony.
He is so scared to let her go,
Without her around, his life will be low.

The years have passed since she was born,
And now from her, his life will be torn.
He will no longer see her face everyday,
She's his pride and joy; she wants him to stay.

But how can he stay in a marriage of no love?
With his little one sacred, as peaceful as a dove.
He can draw her a picture or put lines in the sand,
Of her mummy and daddy, divided they stand.

Into her wee heart will be nothing but pain,
Because her wee world is no longer the same.
How can she be shown what's wrong from right,
When all she sees is her parents fight.

She does not deserve this ritual of sin,
Because in the end, neither one of them will win.
His daughter is so innocent, so precious, so pure,
These ugly onslaughts she needn't endure.

Each breath he inhales, every step that he takes,
Each beat from his heart, every morning he wakes,
He thinks of his daughter with happiness in mind,
How could he ever leave his child behind?

He was the first to hold her within human arms,
Immediately she started to show all her charms.
His little precious angel, he wants you to know,
Your daddy will love you, no matter where he will go.

It is so wrong for your parents to fight,
From early in the morning to the late hours of night.
He knows you can't understand the battles and fuss,
The emotions they portray, the words that they cuss.

And in between them, you make your wee stand,
You try your very best to lend a wee hand.
To correct the problem and become the glue,
Of your mother and father, divided in two.

They have both grown to love you so very, very much,
But now with each other, they have become out of touch.
Their love for you will always remain strong,
Please understand that you have done nothing wrong.

Life is a journey; we follow a path,
Sometimes we cry, sometimes we laugh.
While he sits here now and writes out this poem,
His heart, it is heavy, for you both face the unknown.

Will he get to see your smiling face every day?
Hear the words you recite, watch the fun as you play?
Clean your hands and face after you've eaten so well?
Kiss and tuck you in goodnight with a hug that is swell?

This is the future; he may face it alone,
If he's not with you daily, he'll rely on the phone,
To keep him in touch with his baby so dear,
And right by your side, he will always be near.

You are his own gift, for which he is glad,
You are his wee miracle, and he is your dad.
Never will he feel love again so deep,
That he does with his daughter, who makes his heart leap.

Keep humming the songs you've known for awhile,
For whenever you sing, it makes him smile.
If you ever feel sad, please don't despair,
His baby you are, Daddy will always be there.

Photo by: Michele Parent

Hearts Entwined

Photo by: Karl and Carina Milnes

"Although friends and family may give advice to try and help guide their journey in life, it comes down to the couple to seek that happiness together and work their way through what lies ahead. After all, two different people who have found similar interests and want to spend the rest of their lives together have to bring a balance of equality into the marriage. Regardless of the pressures that life has to offer, finding the time to spend with one another should remain a priority. Being human is to be imperfect, and marriage, just like any other relationship, goes through the ebb and flow of highs and lows."

Through the Eyes of a Belfast Child, page 181.

Hearts Entwined

Our families are gathered, and many a friend,
To witness this blessing, they do descend.
The music begins to our guests' delight,
"Here comes the bride all dressed in white."

We stand at this altar; we desire no fear,
This day we have waited so long to near.
Our will to succeed with the future untold,
We will always feel comfort and never be cold.

Although our days have their ups and downs,
Our smiling lips, they sometimes show frowns.
This adventure we'll challenge as husband and wife,
Stick together we shall through this journey called life.

This day together we are united as one,
To complete our world, never becoming undone.
My heart you are, and forever you'll be,
I am your soul, this you will see.

Take my hand and the rest of me,
Into your life, I forever shall be.
Our hearts combined will beat as one drum,
Will only seek fulfillment and never feel numb.

Our hands are joined in holy matrimony,
Our love is divine, never proving phony.
'Til death do us part is the vow that we keep,
Through the shadows of darkness we never shall sleep.

Every new morning that will look upon us,
Will see us make happiness even when we fuss.
Our moments of sadness will soon fade away,
So long as we are together at the end of each day.

This is our moment, which we celebrate,
Reaching destiny, we've discovered our fate.
In the stars beyond and when we do meet,
Our hearts entwined will continue to beat.

Photo by: StockSnap

Imagine That…

Photo by: Leandro De Carvalho

"How is it that the world's richest countries can spend billions on destructive weapons, yet at the same time, health care is only provided to those who can afford it? And as seen in the housing market crisis in 2009, why are bank executives, who willingly destructed the lives of millions of people and destroyed thousands of dreams due to their own greed, still afforded lucrative bonuses and provided immunity from prosecution?"

Through the Eyes of a Belfast Child, page 147.

Imagine That...

Imagine that you wake up from a dream,
Only to find you are still asleep.
That you believe you are in shallow water,
When it's actually over ten feet.

Imagine that your television is your only friend,
To whom you can always talk.
That the wheelchair in which you sit,
Provides you with the legs to walk.

Imagine that the trigger of the gun you fire,
Will call upon world peace.
That the last payment on your new car,
Is just the start of its lease.

Imagine that when you arrive at work,
You are always sent home with pay.
That you are a motivational speaker,
But do not know what to say.

Imagine that the sun went down,
Although there was always light to shine.
That all forms of money went obsolete,
Yet payphones still required a dime.

Imagine that we were all created equal,
But to each other we were not the same.
That we all went through the journey of life,
Confident in playing the game.

Imagine that you reached your destination,
Yet you haven't boarded the plane.
That you are released from the padded room,
When the white coats know you're insane.

Imagine that when a bank is robbed,
The thieves put the money in the vault.
That with each performed abortion,
The child is born without fault.

Imagine that with the money you've spent,
All of your purchases are free.
That if these words I write were true,
What kind of a world this would be.

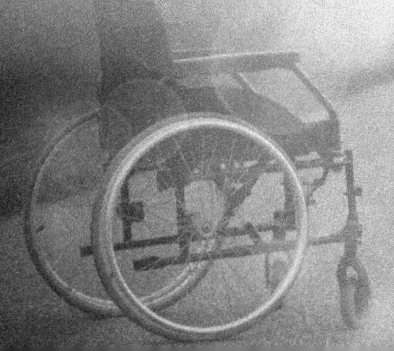

Photo by: Richard Reid

Empty Promises

I'm sorry!

Photo by: Catkm

"Some cultures afford men the right to choose their bride regardless of age. In other religious sects, one man is granted the opportunity to marry a number of women past his first marriage. It begs the question: does the sanctity of marriage not apply in these circles?"

>Through the Eyes of a Belfast Child, page 197.

Empty Promises

On our day of wedding bliss,
These promises I presented to you.
Though now I reflect on the promises we made,
All but one has fallen through.

You promised me you would never leave,
We would only part in death.
All of your promises were sacred words,
While mine were a waste of breath.

I promised you we two were one,
That there would be no other.
But while I gazed into your eyes,
I thought of yet another.

I promised you I would always be there,
Nothing would keep us apart.
Though every day we were together,
'Twas no room for you in my heart.

I promised you when I became angry or mad,
My thoughts would extinguish the fuse.
Although I would not physically assault,
My words would continue the abuse.

I promised I would take care of you,
In sickness and in health.
I promised these words only because,
Your insurance would secure my wealth.

I promised that I would weep for you,
When your time did come to die.
No matter how hard I would force myself,
There were no tears to cry.

The parting words you did fulfill,
With that we were given no choice.
Now that you are finally at peace,
Nevermore will I promise by voice.

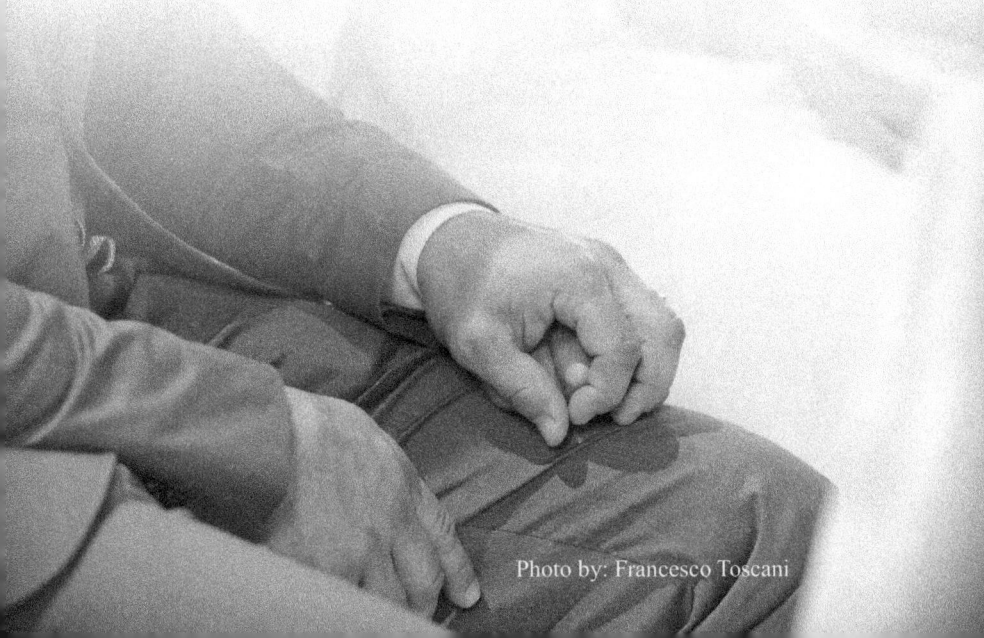

Photo by: Francesco Toscani

Going Forward in Reverse

Photo by: Dagmar Räder

"We are often asked, "Did you get out of the wrong side of the bed this morning?" This may be reflective of a mood, or just that nothing has gone right. Clothes freshly washed and pressed for a corporate presentation fell on the floor during the night, and you have no time to sort them again. The hot water tank has blown, and the day starts off with a cold shower. The alarm clock was set for an early morning interview, only to see that there was a power outage. After filling the dog's bowl with fresh water, dry kibble is absentmindedly put into the same dish. Such events put the day into disarray, and only seem to compound as time goes on. Everything is backwards. It is almost as if someone flipped our left and right brain while we slept. During events such as these, we might just find ourselves wishing for the day to be over, yet it has only just begun."

Through the Eyes of a Belfast Child, page 218.

Going Forward in Reverse

What would you do?
In the middle of the night,
If the moon was dark blue,
And the sky was brilliant white.

Would you fall down to your knees,
Each time someone said please?
Allow them access to your banks,
Every time they said thanks.

When times are extremely hard,
Nothing at all seems funny.
Would you use your credit card,
And spend that plastic money?

Would you try to twiddle your thumb?
Though it's extraordinarily numb.
From that sharp and pointy hook,
Found in a professional fishing book.

Although you're trapped in hell,
When you kneel down ready to pray.
Would you say that you're quite well?
To the man of disarray.

Would you try to write a letter?
Though your printing is no better.
Than when you were in school,
You thought you were so cool.

If your car went on red,
And would not go on green.
Would you stay in bed?
For it caused you quite the scene.

Although you run lightning fast,
Would you take the gum from your shoe?
You finished the race dead last,
Because it stuck to you like glue.

If this is your reflection right now,
It's time to take a bow.
'Cause this is my final verse,
Of you going forward in reverse.

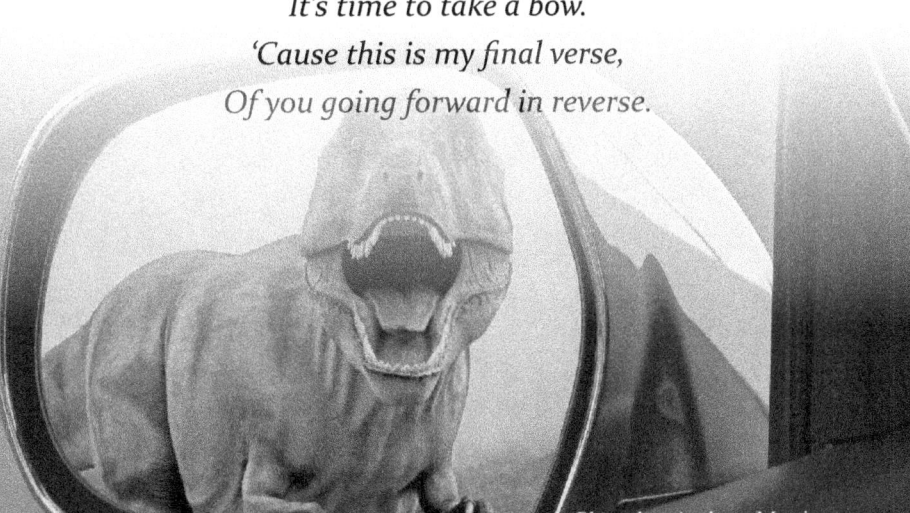

Photo by: Andrew Martin

A New Beginning

Photo by: Jill Wellington

"As a result of learning her story, I was led to question: since when did humans sign all freedoms of their very beings over to someone else to control through the supposed sanctity of marriage regardless of cultural beliefs or social standing? It made me realize that when one partner is being controlled within a relationship and recognizes that life is no longer in their own hands but is dictated to them by the very person in whom they instilled their trust, love, and respect through the "obey and serve" ideology, the fight for human survival begins."

Through the Eyes of a Belfast Child, page 165.

A New Beginning

I am a person, and someone I know,
My only true friend is not my foe,
I walk with me in every stride,
My head held high with tremendous pride.

I poured out my soul; I gave all that I had,
In return for my compassion, they said I was mad,
Whether I was awake or as I did sleep,
Into my spirit they drove daggers so deep.

While walking upon me, they poisoned my veins,
They filled me with drink and cast me in chains,
To my own true self, I became such a stranger,
I did not realize that my life was in danger.

The anger inside me has started to burn,
My life is taking a sudden turn,
I'll let this fuel my inner fire,
I'll use the flame to my heart's desire.

This raging inferno that lies so deep within,
Will only be doused with whiskey and gin,
My mind will be dulled and become quite numb,
Allowing others to place me under their thumb.

Others will say my love is so blind,
These others are ignorant, this they will find,
I'll be taken no more as a fool for a wife,
A fresh start I've been granted in this wonderful life.

If my spirit stays strong, I will then see,
I'm the controller of my own destiny,
Those who scratch and claw at my skin,
Will begin to realize that they never shall win.

Although my kinfolk are so far away,
Our hands are entwined with each waking day,
Without ever thinking each time that I breathe,
You walk by my side; you never shall leave.

Your eyes were swollen from the tears you cried,
We saw your inner flame, having almost died,
So be kind to thyself and make a new start,
You have to believe within your own heart.

Creator sits high with pieces from your mold,
Great Spirit did well when creating your soul.
This shaped your being and so we are told,
With principles so high, they can never be sold.

Its time you realized to your own self be true,
Without your strengths, whatever would they do?
These words we share, these words we recite,
Will protect you each morning and comfort you at night.

So before you kneel down ready to pray,
Look in the mirror and to yourself say,
"I'll be filled with such happiness, no room for old strife,
Tomorrow will be the best day of my life."

No longer sigh heavy; no longer despair,
Your heart is now on the road to repair,
Your energy will strengthen and never divide,
Your flame will glow brightly and for others provide.

The courage they need to overcome fright,
To guide them from evil and lead them to light,
To conquer all anguish, to learn how to laugh,
They will follow so closely, in your chosen path.

If ever you are gripped by an unwelcome fear,
The shadows of darkness will soon disappear,
Our love and kindness will fill you with pride,
New beginnings you'll have, we're here by your side.

The Pulse of Derrylin

Photo by: Jamil Ahsan

"The concert was brilliant, but we were terrified, as it was rumored that during the song "Freedom Fighters," the divide we lived through was part of the show. We understood that Protestants in the audience would go to one side of the venue, Catholics to the other, and they would charge each other before meeting in the middle and getting into a full-blown war while the concert would play on."

Through the Eyes of a Belfast Child, page 112.

The Pulse of Derrylin

I sit here ready to write about,
Three young lads from Fermanagh I know.
Music they created when called Pulse,
Made many people's hearts glow.

These three lads that I speak about,
Started their careers quite young.
Playing the delicate music of Ireland,
At Fleadh Cheoils just for fun.

Suddenly all things in their careers would change,
Upon witnessing their first Horslips show.
The McManus brothers stood back in amazement,
When O'Connor played fiddle and bow.

The lads told their parents this show was so terrible,
They couldn't hear music, just noise.
Who'd ever guess that bearing witness to this,
Would form the Pulse of Mama's Boys.

Arriving home as they did at the end of each gig,
Their parents would ask the same.
If these shows are so terrible, so bad, and so boring,
How come you go every night in the rain?

Their names I can quote quite easily,
Tommy, John, and Pat The Professor.
Taking their lessons from the lads of Thin Lizzy,
And Horslips, Irish rock music's predecessor.

For John, the voice, the Uilleann pipes would not do,
Now he ran at a sprinter's pace.
His eyes locked upon his father so dear,
When he arrived home with the family's first bass.

Tommy, the bodhrán player, ever steady with the beat,
Was now also interested in new tunes.
His father decided it was time for some drums,
Instead of beating cushions with spoons.

Pat the Professor not to be forgotten,
Would prove he was a rising star.
Although he'd nick Johnny Fean's ideas,
He chose to play bow on guitar.

To the stage the brothers would take,
Singing songs derived from rock 'n' roll.
Adding Irish music to their newfound rhythms,
All the while playing from heart and soul.

Around the pubs in Ireland,
They toured themselves quite well.
Placing each fan in the crowd,
Under a euphoric spell.

To them it was never a problem,
How many fans came to the show.
As soon as the lights went down,
Mama's Boys were raring to go.

As a matter of fact,
It did not take long.
For their following to grow,
To hundreds and thousands strong.

For these brothers were very different,
In the way their music was played.
Always smiling while up on the stage,
Their faces never looking dismayed.

Over the days and throughout the years,
They sung out their songs with passion.
John learned while touring with Thin Lizzy,
That Phil Lynott's legwarmers were in fashion.

Sadly our happiness would suddenly change;
Tommy was called with a whisper in the breeze.
Fans found out that he was now drumming in heaven,
In sorrow, friends fell to their knees.

The rock world was stunned with this heartbreaking news,
Now the future for us all was uncertain.
Tommy made mention that if he were called to his maker,
With Phil Lynott he would draw a new curtain.

Looking down on us all, especially his family,
Tommy would not let this legacy come to an end.
His rhythm it beats within The Professor and John,
Now with Celtus, our hearts will mend.

Photo by: Jamil Ahsan

Mum's Lament

Photo by: Greg McVicker

"Some of my mum's last words to me before she passed were, "Greg, I'm not getting out of this hospital. I'm not coming home." I reassured her that she was coming home and that she would indeed be in her house again. Little did I realize that my words would be true: we brought her back for her wake to celebrate her beautiful and courageous life under the cloak of death."

Through the Eyes of a Belfast Child, page 131.

Mum's Lament

Our mother's love so special,
As many folks can see.
Mum's greatest gift was giving life,
To my sisters, brother, and me.

We began as children so helpless, Mum,
Yet never a challenge for you.
No matter how little or large the task,
There's nothing you couldn't do.

Throughout the years and as we grew,
So proud of us you were.
If we needed something, Mum,
We knew you'd always be there.

You gave us so much precious love,
Which came from deep inside.
Knowing the amazing Mum you are,
Fills us with tremendous pride.

You steered us through our battles, Mum,
No one can disagree.
You guided us in darkened times,
And now we set you free.

You taught us so much wisdom, Mum,
And loved us with your heart.
A new journey you shall now begin,
For a little while we must part.

Mum, our time with you was far too short,
There's much we'd like to say.
The days ahead they are unknown,
Without you leading the way.

Although you'll look down upon us, Mum,
And incredibly sad, we'll fuss.
We take great pride in the fact that,
Your blood flows proudly through us.

Mum, we share your strengths instilled in us,
Knowing what we must do.
To continue the legacy you've already begun,
While lovingly remembering you.

Sail gently into the night, our love,
Your new beginning has come.
Although at this moment we say farewell,
Forever you are our Mum.

A wee message from Daddy too:
Kathleen, my sweet precious angel, a loving mum.
Tiocfaidh Ár Lá,
(Our day will come).

Mum, Dad is our sailor, you are our captain and ship,
And we, your children, are your crew.
With everlasting love and fondest memories,
until we meet again,
Karen, Joseph, Gregory, and Angela.

Go n-éirí an t-ádh leat agus go mbeannaí Dia dhuit, Mum.
(Good luck and God bless).

Photo by: Michele de Santis

"I attended the funeral, which was heartbreaking. As any parent can attest, a child can obviously touch the lives of everyone who has had the pleasure of meeting or knowing them. We spend every waking minute worrying about their wellbeing, making sure they are fed, clothed, and take care of their every need such as cleaning scraped knees, applying ice to bruises, kissing their owee's better, and giving them a warm hug before tucking them in at bedtime. We play roles as Santa, the Tooth Fairy, and the Easter Bunny for our children."

Through the Eyes of a Belfast Child, page 191.

Lament for a Child

The day started out with heartache,
Knowing what we had to do.
Make our way to the service,
And bid a fond farewell to you.

Your pictures up upon the screen,
Countless tears did fall.
The lives and hearts your love has filled,
Echoed through the hall.

No one could have prepared us,
In our time to say goodbye.
Creator called you to heaven,
Sweet angel in the sky.

We saw the signs you sent today,
And counted them: one, two, three.
You wanted to show everyone,
"Hey look, I am still among thee."

The dragonfly within the crowd,
It touched each one of us.
"It's me, your little angel,
So please don't make a fuss.

I fly so free amongst you all,
Look up into the sky.
I'm one of the birds you now see,
It's not time to say goodbye.

The warmth you feel upon your face,
As provided by the sun.
Shhh... it's really me sending my love,
To each and every one.

I'll see you someday in heaven,
And will come to play with you.
That blinking star in the sky,
It's me winking back at you.

Although our time was short,
And now we have to part.
I will always be your precious child,
I'll live on within your heart."

Surreal, Nine One One

Photo by: Gerd Altmann

"I've heard many people recollect where they were on the day when John F. Kennedy, the thirty-fifth President of the United States of America, was shot dead in 1963. Others may choose to remember when it was announced that Elvis Presley had died in 1977. There are those who recall when John Lennon was killed outside his New York apartment in 1980. Honestly, I never knew any of these events, as John F. Kennedy was killed seven years before I was born. Elvis died seven years after. I did not know who the Beatles were until much later in life."

Through the Eyes of a Belfast Child, page 214.

Surreal, Nine One One

While I sit, my eyes are glued to TV,
Horrifying images reflect back at me.
Unable to move, I'm in disbelief,
America attacked; the whole world is in grief.

Innocent people from all walks of life,
Tried to give help to comrades in strife.
Lifeless beings now trapped in a cell,
The World Trade Center has turned into hell.

These scenes I view, could this be a dream?
Deep down inside I just want to scream.
It seems so surreal, like a deadly nightmare,
I open my eyes and continue to stare.

Brave men and women, their hands they lent,
To rescue others was their intent.
A courageous search on a crumpled floor,
The towers collapse, their lives no more.

I watch so many, they shout and cry,
Thousands did not deserve to die.
While I stare at my screen, I kneel and pray,
For America to see light at the end of the day.

Although right now the world feels numb,
Those responsible, they have not won.
We are a nation and we stand free,
God Bless America, please God, bless me.

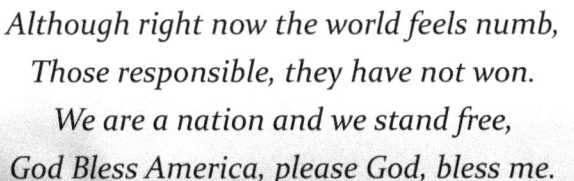

Photo by: Pixabay Member 12019

Bruised and Battered

Photo by: Alrike Mai

"Unfortunately, I have friends who are in this exact predicament and have literally suffered in complete silence for years from the abuses they continue to undergo. They, along with others I do not know, feel that they have made their decision and are to live and die by them. They are terrified to leave their abusers, and in having suffered so many years of psychological trauma, feel completely worthless and undeserving of a better life and remain in a negative environment."

Through the Eyes of a Belfast Child, page 202.

Bruised and Battered

Welcoming him home from work,
She promised his favourite meal.
Offered a kiss before she cooked,
    A dish of breaded veal.

It wasn't what he wanted,
Telling her to get out of his face.
He'd already had a rough day,
Plenty more work yet to chase.

She stated her apology,
And offered to make things right.
Sweetly she asked, "Will you join me,
In a bubble bath tonight?"

His response, as sharp as daggers,
"I've so much more to do!
Countless deadlines to meet,
Wasted dollars supporting you."

"Baby, you know I miss you," she sobbed,
"We never share quality time.
Is loving you deeply as I do,
Such a terrible crime?"

"What's wrong with you?" he screamed,
"Will you quit annoying me?
Once again you're under my skin,
Making me so very angry!"

"But honey, I love you so much!" she did cry,
"When not with you, I'm sad.
I only wanted to ensure your happiness,
I didn't mean to make you mad."

His rising hand, it slapped her face,
She fell like a lump of lard.
"Oh baby, can't you see I'm sorry,
I didn't mean to hit you so hard."

**Her crumpled body upon the floor,
Her rosy cheek did sting.
Her trembling hand covering the bruise,
Left there by his high school ring.**

Kneeling down onto the floor,
As he looked her in the eye.
"Baby, I really didn't mean it this time,"
One hand upon his fly.

She knew his sorrow meant nothing,
As her head began to throb.
He grabbed a handful of golden hair,
Her mouth began to bob.

"Baby, you know I really do love you,
When you take good care of me."
He would not let go of his grasp,
Until she had finished he.

Paralyzed by all her fear,
She asked, "Baby, did that feel good?"
Hoping just as she always did,
Her deed would lighten the mood.

"That makes things so much better,
Let's continue on with our day.
Good thing you know what best for you,"
He muttered while walking away.

As she rose up from the floor,
She prayed that it would end.
"Some day when I will find the strength,
My broken heart will mend."

Sitting back down at his desk,
His actions now in the past.
"Hey, when am I getting my dinner?
You'd better make it real fast."

She went to fix his plate,
And brought to him his meal.
"How did you know what I wanted?" he asked,
Upon seeing the breaded veal.

Many years have since passed;
Her heart remains broken and shattered.
Her pain hidden behind a fractured smile,
Her face still bruised and battered.

Photo by: Österreich

Disposable Human

Photo by: Peter Gottschalk

"As a student, I learned of a high-profile individual in one Canadian city who would buy oral pleasures from sex trade workers. Fifteen dollars was merely pocket change to the judge, but to the women fulfilling his request, they could buy another substance hit to fill their veins. Within two weeks though, the judge would often see these same women in his courtroom and blast them as being a disgrace to society, as being nothing more than dirt and filth and lucky he did not throw the book at them. Did these thoughts cross his mind upon reaching orgasm?"

Through the Eyes of a Belfast Child, page 210.

Disposable Human

A broken life, a broken home,
Out on the streets I dwell.
In order to survive each night alone,
My body I hate to sell.

But living out here, I have no choice,
To keep myself alive.
Crack, cocaine, and heroin,
My friends help me survive.

Strangers lurk within the dark,
Begging service for a fee.
Roughly, they enter my body,
No love for whom they see.

For all I am is disposable,
In the minds of those I please.
They do not see me as human,
Nothing more than just a sleaze.

So do not look into my eyes,
Or question for my name.
Dump yourself inside my soul,
And leave me with your shame.

You really are no different,
From each trick I've met before.
Take me, pay me, use me,
And kick me out the door.

I'll pick up all the pieces,
Once you've done your filthy deed.
Now awaiting my next customer,
To fulfill their sexual need.

This cycle will repeat itself,
All throughout the night.
Dirty money within my hand,
Will soon be gone from sight.

Although my life is broken,
My home was filled with pain.
Please note I'm someone's daughter,
Before you seek me out again.

Photo by: Alexandr Ivanov

The Confessional

Photo by: James Chan

"Sure enough, when attending my first year of class, I watched more than enough times as young men around my age were fondled, groped, sexually violated, and exploited on a repeated basis while we were supposed to be learning our mother tongue. The name given to the brother should have been that of "a friggin' pedophile," as that is exactly what he was, preying on the flesh of young and unsuspecting boys."

        Through the Eyes of a Belfast Child, page 58.

The Confessional

In the Name of the Father,
And of the Son,
Dear God, forgive me,
For the sins I have done.

Although not a priest,
But a Christian brother.
Behind my rosary,
I place my cover.

I covet my pupils,
Allow them no choice.
With the Celtic language,
I teach them their voice.

They are my boys,
I love them so dear.
When they speak to me,
I respond, "Come here."

My hands they wander,
To capture a feel.
Those pretty young boys,
I ask them to kneel.

Look up at me, child,
For I want you to know.
Open your mouth wide,
My seed I will sow.

Once I am done,
Wipe your lips dry.
Keep this our secret,
My child, do not cry.

God will bless you,
For this deed you have done.
You're free to go,
Thank you, my son.

Who will be next?
In front of my chair.
Praise to you, Lord,
Hear my prayer.

Photo by: James Chan

Acknowledgements

I'd like to acknowledge a few people who have inspired me to no end throughout the years.

Karen McVicker, my beloved and cherished sister. After being diagnosed in September 2011 with Acute Lymphoblastic Leukaemia, she waged a courageous and determined battle that only a Celtic Warrior could do to defeat this life-threatening disease. Although successful in those efforts and without ever questioning why she was given the monumental challenge to do so, she relapsed.

In the face of adversity, she fought right through to her final day until she was called to join our mum. You spent forty-eight years on this earth, a timeframe that was far too young. Those lucky enough to be enriched by your worldview and knowledge should certainly count their blessings.

Rest In Peace, sis. Karen, I love you, I miss you, and as I have said before, only the Creator knows how much my heart breaks each and every day...

Caitlin and **Ciarán McVicker**, my children, who have inspired me to no end. I am honoured to be their dad. I've often said as adults, we have our biases determined and worldviews set. However, when looking at life from our children's perspective, and through the innocence of their eyes, it creates a new awakening. Embrace your Irish heritage, for it is truly a blessing.

Finally, I would like to extend a personal heartfelt thank you to the following individuals for their photos which have added a phenomenal, yet intense dimension to the narrative poems within this book. With the exception of Ciarán, Caitlin, Jamil, Karl, Carina, and myself, all images were sourced through www.pixabay.com to which these talented artists are dedicated contributors. Each of them deserves full acknowledgment for their outstanding efforts, and in making their images available to the community at large:

Ciarán McVicker, Caitlin McVicker, Florian Pircher, Patricia Alexandre, Christine Zimmer, Enrique Meseguer, Patrice Audet, Anthony, degreezero, Khusen Rustamov, Stefan Keller, Gerd Altmann, Sally Wynn, Michele Parent, Karl and Carina Milnes, Leandro De Carvalho, Richard Reid, Catkin, Francesco Toscani, Dagmar Räder, Andrew Martin, Jill Wellington, Jamil Ahsan, Michele de Santis, Alrike Mai, Österreich, Peter Gottschalk, Alexandr Ivanov, James Chan, and to the three artists who simply go by nothing more than their Pixabay Member Numbers: 3345408, 733215, and 12019.

Sláinte mhaith! Cheers!

Other Titles from Greg McVicker

Through the Eyes of a Belfast Child:
Life. Personal Reflections. Poems.

First Edition   - May 2014
Second Edition - November 2017

"This is totally fantastic! Even the wee poems were such a pleasure to read. This is something I'd read again and again. Above all, I'm sure your mammy is looking down on you with such pride and love. I have never read such beautiful words written by anyone to describe their mum as you have. The feelings are there, but putting them into words is something else. I actually filled up reading some parts, a wee mixture of smiles and tears. I'm sure that anyone else who reads this will react exactly the same. Not only have you put a lot of hard work and time into this, you've also written this with your heart."

- Teresa McAuley.
Belfast, County Antrim, Northern Ireland.

ISBN: 978-1-7751622-8-5 (Hardcover)
              978-1-7751622-6-1 (Softcover)
              978-1-7751622-7-8 (eBook)

One Cross to Bear:
Humanity Through Narrative Prose

First Edition – October 23, 2017

"Using his distinctive style of storytelling by way of stanza and prose, Irish Poet and Author, Greg McVicker, dives headfirst into the turbulent cycle of life. In "One Cross to Bear", his latest collection of poetry, he takes us on a whirlwind journey of his years growing up in his native Northern Ireland, up to the present day in Canada. Poems such as; "Belfast City Asylum" and "Everlasting Homesickness" paint a vivid picture of growing up in war-torn Belfast, and the pain he endured at being torn away from all that he knew in order to start a new life in a safer, but foreign land. Greg writes unashamedly from the heart, reaching out to his readers and carrying them along the waves of an emotional tsunami. I have no doubt that these poetic stories have and will continue to affect untold numbers of individuals throughout their lifetime."

- J.P. Sexton, Author of;
'The Big Yank – Memoir of a Boy Growing Up Irish.'

ISBN: 978-1-7751622-3-0 (eBook)
978-1-989053-18-8 (Softcover)

The Adventures of Silly Billy:
Silly Billy and the Postage Stamp

First Edition   – January 14, 2015
   (eBook)

Second Edition – May 3, 2016
   (Softcover)

Third Edition   – November 2017

Silly Billy and the Postage Stamp:
In this first adventure, and since his father is away at sea, Billy wants to be like his older brother who assumes the role of being the "Man of the House", and bosses his siblings around. Given a simple task of mailing a letter to their father, this comical true-life story which is set in the community of Newtownabbey, Northern Ireland, captures the childhood experiences of Irish Author and Poet, Greg McVicker, in how one young boy can take a simple task and make a complete mess of it. The moral of this story is to not try covering up ones' countless mistakes and mishaps along the way as eventually they will be found out.

ISBN: 978-1-7751622-5-4 (eBook)
               978-1-989053-19-5 (Softcover)

The Adventures of Silly Billy:
Silly Billy and the Good Deed

First Edition   – May 17, 2016
(Softcover)
Second Edition – November 2017

Silly Billy and the Good Deed:

In this second adventure, and since the tuck shop at his primary school is all sold out, Billy is asked to help his teacher get her favourite sweets along with his own reward. However, what should have taken only a few moments becomes an amusing escapade that is filled with numerous misfortunes due to Billy not following very specific directions. This hilarious true-life story which takes place in Newtownabbey, Northern Ireland, captures the childhood experiences of Irish Author and Poet, Greg McVicker, and his memories from years gone by. The moral of this story is to try your best, but to also do as one is told to do in the first place.

ISBN: 978-1-7751622-5-4 (eBook)
                978-1-989053-19-5 (Softcover)

The Adventures of Silly Billy:
Silly Billy and the Escape from Carrick Castle

First Edition – **November 2017**

Silly Billy and the Escape from Carrick Castle:

In this third adventure, Billy is offered a chance to go fishing with his older brother and his mates alongside of the marina beside a Norman castle built in 1177 on the northern shores of Belfast Lough in Carrickfergus. Once there, however, fishing seems to be the last thing on their minds and leads to a troublesome chase within the confines of this mighty structure. This hysterical true-life reflection which took place in Newtownabbey, Northern Ireland, captures the childhood experiences of Irish Author and Poet, Greg McVicker. The moral of this story is that your freedom might not quite be your fate, especially when your father comes home.

ISBN: 978-1-7751622-5-4 (eBook)
978-1-989053-19-5 (Softcover)

Connect with the Author

I would love to hear your story, for who knows what kind of higher learning or healing can come from it, or how it can help support someone else by knowing that they are not alone in their journey of life.

If you are interested in connecting with me, please feel free to do so. I make every effort to respond to all enquiries within a timely manner, and certainly look forwards to hearing from you!

facebook: ThroughtheEyesofaBelfastChild
email: gmcvicker70@gmail.com
twitter: @BelfastChild70
hashtag: #BelfastChild

www.ingramcontent.com/pod-product-compliance
Lightning Source LLC
Chambersburg PA
CBHW032137040426
42449CB00005B/291